That One Time, With Prince

Andrew Kistner

To my beautiful wife, Jyotiee

THAT ONE TIME, WITH PRINCE
CONTENTS

Introduction

Sometimes there is a joke in Minnesota when I tell someone that I used to work for Prince... it goes like this: "Who hasn't?"... Other than trying to burst my bubble, there is a reason this "joke" came about. A lot of employees came and went from Paisley Park. In fact, Prince had a reputation for turning over staff quite often. I had seen a lot of people come and go but somehow I lasted. I was a naive, small town kid who didn't know much about him. Perhaps that was somehow refreshing for an international icon.

After he died, I started seeing a lot of people share their Prince stories... both employees and celebrities. Some stories I believed and some I did not. It made me realize that I took for granted how much of an influence he had on people. This brought back many memories and I recognized that I had a very unique experience... Not many people had spent the amount of time with Prince as I had.

I really didn't have a title at Paisley Park... Basically an hourly employee of the studio. I was the quiet guy who didn't seek a lot of credit for things. I think that's why I lasted so long... five years is a lengthy Prince career... and I was there during the time of a skeleton crew where, many times you ended up working directly with Prince.

Paisley Park was not too far from the small town where I grew up. I honestly did not pay too much attention to Prince and I was never really a fan. I had never seen Purple Rain. I knew very little of his fight with the record label... I didn't even know he played guitar. Then in high school I got a job working for a lawn care service where Paisley Park and Prince's house were two of the accounts we mowed. I started with this lawn care company when I was 16 years old and the closest I would get to Prince is a rare occasion where he would drive past me in one of his cars with limo-tinted glass. Even with him behind these black, reflective windows, I would try not to look, thinking back to the stories about people being so easily fired.

After high school, I went off to college to study graphic design. When I came back for the summer, I called my lawn care boss and asked when I could start working again. He proceeded to tell me that he had quit the business and got hired as "estate manager" at Paisley Park. He mentioned that if any opportunities for work came up, he would let me know.

A month or so passed and he called me to say that there was some work available. He said that it was only going to be about a 3-month project, turning the loading dock into a live music venue/club... I had no idea that 3 months would turn into over five years. I would work at Paisley and go out on tour, as well.

Traveling the world with an international music legend was very valuable experience that not many people will ever have. At the time, I did not realize how influential Prince was. With his death, I really got an idea of how many people my old boss touched through his music. I found that many people are fascinated by the man and that's why I decided to share some of my old stories.

Hopefully after reading the following, you will have an idea of what it was like for a small town kid to get thrown into the world of an international rock star.

1
WHEN IT WAS MY FIRST DAY ON THE JOB

I was a 19-year-old kid, driving a tan Chevy S-10 with garbage piled everywhere in it. My Paisley journey began when I took this trusty little truck from my small town in rural Minnesota and drove into the western suburbs of Minneapolis. I arrived at Paisley Park for my first day of work. I was met by my old, lawn-care boss from high school who had gotten me the job. He showed me around the back of the building, where I would be working. The job was going to be manual labor, helping to turn the loading dock into a live music venue.

I remember being not-too-impressed... I can't say for sure what I expected... maybe a Prince-version of Willy Wonka's factory with purple lacy frills everywhere? Whatever it was that I expected... it was

5

not that. The back of the building had a cold, concrete floor with storage areas made from chain link fence and a couple sets of industrial metal stairs. This was literally a loading dock. It looked like it was the back of a widget manufacturing plant, not an international superstar's personal recording studio. It was very anticlimactic.

My old lawn care boss showed me around and introduced me to the person I'd be working with. I am not sure which tour had just finished but the guy was the production manager. He was staying at the Chanhassen Inn, temporarily working at Paisley. Sometimes Prince would have his "road guys" do work at the studio. He directed me on what to do and brought up the fact that I might see Prince around. His advice for me was: "If he comes into the room, just act like he's not there". I was supposed to go on with my work and not pay any attention to him.

These were not official Paisley Park rules passed down from Prince (and I was actually expecting to hear something like that). It was simply advice from a guy who wanted to keep some reliable help.

This would be the start of a five year journey with my new, eccentric-millionaire, rock star boss.

2
WHEN YOU COULD NOT SPEAK TO HIM

This was when there was still a receptionist/admin at the front desk of Paisley Park (I think I was there for the last one). I'm pretty sure I had been there less than a year but Prince had seen me around enough to know that I was a full-time employee. Also, less-than-a-year was long enough to know that sometimes he could have a pretty intense persona. I had even noticed that some people would avoid him if they could.

   That's why I got a little nervous when the receptionist called me up to the front desk. He wanted me to give Prince a package. It was his copy of "Muppets Tonight" when he was the guest star. When the guy at the front desk asked, I must have given him a look like he was crazy. He smirked and went on to tell me "It's no big deal... just walk up to him and give it to him".

I remember being horribly nervous. I had never really been a Prince fan before I worked out there (When I first started, people would talk about Wendy and Lisa... I thought they were women who used to work in an office at Paisley, like accountants). So, I wasn't nervous because he was Prince, I was nervous because he was this weird, mysterious, eccentric guy that was the boss at my new job. Growing up in Minnesota, I had heard stories about how you got fired if you looked at him... now I have to walk right up to him and interrupt him while he is relaxing.

So, it was time to find out what happens when you talk to him... I headed toward the kitchen where I approached him. I had not yet said anything and he looked at me. It was the same look that I'd see many times after that. The look that seemed to say "This better be quick and important"... I told him that I was supposed to give this to him. He asked what it was and I said it was from "The Muppets". He grabbed the show tape and gave me back a letter they wrote to him... he didn't say anything but there was another "look"... This one said "You should know better than to give me this extra crap I don't need".

I jammed the letter in my pocket when he asked me to do something else. It's hard to recall but I think he wanted me to find someone and send them to the kitchen.

Prince had a powerful presence… It is very difficult to explain. He had a piercing look used in a lot of non-verbal communication. I learned to interpret these looks pretty well. They would precede many conversations, letting me know whether or not he was available to talk.

Andrew Kistner

3
WHEN YOU LITERALLY COULD NOT SAY HIS NAME

Having not been a Prince fan, I did not know the details of the dispute between him and the record company. Of course I knew it caused him to change his name to the symbol. You would've had to have been living under a rock to be unaware of that. One of the most common questions I was asked when I worked with him was "What do you call him?"... because he literally had an unpronounceable symbol for his name.

There were actually a number of different ways that employees got his attention. The most common was simply approaching him and just look like you had something to say. He'd give you a look back to let you know if he was available to talk or not... If you were in a situation where you had to get his attention... like when you'd call a normal person by their very useful name, which he did not have... most people would simply address him as "sir".

This moniker worked well enough, except when you would get a stubborn roadie who would huff and puff about it... normally they would be very outspoken about not calling him "sir". This was to assure that we all knew they were not a beta male to Prince's alpha status (There is usually no shortage of egos in the music business). These were mainly people on tour that did not travel back home to Paisley once the tour has ended.

There was also a difference while referencing him when he wasn't around... Almost all the time it was "boss"... This was actually a title Prince did not like. There was a time on tour where the sound man said something like "Can you bring me Boss's microphone?"

When Prince heard this, he immediately announced "I'm not your boss. I'm your co-worker". The sound man was quick enough to come back with "Can you bring me Coworker's microphone?"... Everybody had a good laugh and I think Prince appreciated the quick comeback.

You would also see sign-language for his name... If someone walked past you and held their hand to their chest, referencing his stature, most likely somewhere behind that guy, you would see Prince… Or perhaps over one of the production radios you hear the phrase "Your package has arrived"… Guess what? Yep… purple guy.

I worked there long enough for him to change his name back to Prince. However, I don't even think I ever called him Prince to his face in five years. My preferred way to get his attention was to just walk up to him, then from years of experience, decipher whichever "look" he gave me.

Andrew Kistner

4
WHEN I PUSHED HIM AROUND ON
A BOX CART

Believe it or not, a big part of being a Paisley Park employee was moving things... and when I say "things", I don't mean it was all symbol-shaped guitars and Grammy awards (although sometimes it was). I mean it was mainly boxes... the boring, cardboard kind. There were multiple times while working there when the soundstage went from empty, to full of storage, then to half-empty, then full, then empty. I think you get it... there was lots of box-moving.

I don't know if you've ever worked a job where you had to move boxes. If not, you'll never know the importance of a nice 2-wheel dolly. Trust me, they come in all kinds of different quality levels... and at Paisley, we had one of the good ones. It folded down and went from a 2-wheeler to a 4-wheeler. It was the complete package for all of your box-moving needs. It also "kind of" worked for wheeling Prince around.

This was the late 90's when professional quality digital video cameras were becoming more easily available. Prince bought one and at the time, it was top of the line. With this camera, we could shoot profession quality video without calling in an entire crew. Sometimes Prince, himself would like to get on the shooting-end of this new toy.

It was very late at night and we were working on shooting footage for a music video. I can't remember what song but it was for one of the Paisley Park side-project bands. Prince could recognize talent and was known to help out some smaller groups... very hands-on, both in the studio and obviously while shooting a music video.

As the evening goes on, Prince asks me if I've seen the tracks that get laid down for moving camera shots in a film production. I was vaguely familiar (and still don't know what they're called)... but I had seen them before, both at Paisley Park and on TV... I told him that I "pretty much know" what they are. Then he said that he wanted to get a shot like that. He pointed at the box-moving dolly (which was folded down into 4-wheeler mode) and said "let's use that".

I wasn't much for asking questions when Prince said to do something, so I grabbed it and brought it over... If it was your first time seeing one of these dollies, I'm sure you'd say "Wow, what a super-efficient way to move boxes". With that being said, I am double-sure you would NOT say "Wow, I bet that thing is super easy to squat down on and ride while someone else pushes it".

It's a rare occasion when I will call another man graceful... but having seen Prince perform probably a thousand times (no kidding) I think he is deserving of that description. Even Prince, in all his gracefulness could not make it look easy climbing onto that cart. It was pretty awkward as you heard the clank! clank! clank! of high heels against the cart's metal frame.

When he finally got situated, I gave him the camera and he started to direct the action. As I began pushing the cart, he was actually heavier than I thought he would be. It was an awkward push to get him started and I remember looking up and seeing a couple people with a petrified look that seemed to say "Oh $#*&!, he's gonna kill this guy!" It looked like they were all crouched and ready to pounce in anticipation of saving Prince in a box cart wreck.

The anticipated wreck never happened but as I think back, this was one of the weirdest things that I've ever done in my life... having one of the most influential artists in music history ask to get himself loaded up onto a box cart and have me push him around... If you're a "one-upper" story teller, you'll have to bring your A-game against this one

Everyone in that room, including Prince knew that camera shot would not turn out but it didn't matter... because in my eyes, as a visual artist myself, having fun and experimenting are fundamentals of learning a craft. That night I got to see Prince incorporate those fundamentals into a video shoot. It was a night where he was not a worldwide superstar but I got to see him in my eyes truly as an "artist".

5
WHEN THERE WAS A BREACH IN VEGETARIAN SECURITY

If someone took a poll of all Americans, I think 90% of people would answer "yes" to the following question: Have you ever met a preachy vegetarian?

I am in that majority and I have met multiple throughout my life, one of them being Prince. It is no secret that the music icon felt so strongly about his meatless philosophy. He would announce to 10,000 fans at a time in concert that the only things with eyes they should eat are potatoes. Eventually, being meat-free turned into a day-to-day routine on tour. Our hired caterers would only prepare vegetarian food and at one point, there was no meat allowed at Paisley Park.

There was a time when a painter was doing some airbrushing at the studio and it caused the smoke alarms to go off occasionally. I was walking past the kitchen during one of these times and Prince jokingly yelled out to everyone within earshot that it was the "meat alarm".

Nowadays I do better with veggies than I used to but on tour I really struggled with all-vegetarian food. I was in heaven when the caterers would leave the toaster out all day with peanut butter and jelly... Don't get me wrong the food was good... but it was almost "too good". The caterers would always work hard to make a gourmet veggie dish. For me, they would have been better off with grilled cheese and tomato soup. Eventually, I started taking walks to the arena concourses, just as the doors opened for fans. I would have full access to all of the arena concession stands and all the meat-junk-food that I could eat.

I don't recall the specific city but I was riding down the backstage elevator with 2 hot dogs, minding my own business when the doors opened and I started to walk out... yep... you guessed it, Prince was right there. There was absolutely no way for me to hide these contraband tube steak treasures from him and he saw me turn white as a ghost as my brain scrambled with thoughts about what I should do.

I had flashbacks to hearing stories about Paul McCartney firing people for eating meat on his tour.

Would I be sent home for eating a lousy hot dog? To my surprise, Prince did not say anything. He completely let me off the hook for blatantly disregarding his no-meat request... For some reason, I got a free pass.

There is one other person I know of who got a free pass for eating meat on Prince's watch... This was back at Paisley and he was one of the coolest, nicest, down-to-earth celebrities that I met. He made such a great impression that I will never forget for the rest of my life... George Clinton.

I'm not sure if anyone told him about the policy at Paisley but he sat down in Prince's kitchen and started having a chicken dinner from the local grocery store. There was a buzz around the back of the building; the crew was wondering if Prince was going to bust him and sound the "meat alarm"... nope... Mr. P-Funk got to finish his dinner in peace without interruption.

I had seen Prince sometimes be a very difficult boss and I know that certain people would not have lasted if they completely disregarded his rules. One thing I can take with me for the rest of my life is that I was granted the same pardon as a funk legend for whom Prince had the utmost respect.

6
WHEN I GAVE ANI DIFRANCO HER FAVORITE 4TH OF JULY

I grew up in a small town with a population of about 2000 people. There was one stoplight when I was growing up and I felt a little sad when I saw it is now gone. I'll skip any more of the sentimental memories and Garrison Keillor- esque anecdotes... but I will say that many times it was pretty quiet.

As you can guess, in my small-town upbringing I had never really personally met a celebrity. Then when I turned 19, I started to work for Prince. In the 5+ years I was there, I had seen famous people scattered throughout. Some were nice, some were not and with some I never got the chance to interact. I recall the time when Ani Difranco came to the studio to collaborate with Prince.

It was a day when I didn't see much of Prince. We were working on something in the back of the building while Prince and Ani were at the front, in the recording studio. It was the 4th of July and for the entire day I had plans to go to the roof and watch fireworks. I can sometimes be an easily excitable guy and this was one of those times. Finally, dusk was approaching and soon the sun would be down and my highly anticipated event would start.

I made the decision that I would not keep it to myself. I walked to the front of the building and the timing worked out well where Prince and Ani were taking a short break. I brought up the rooftop-fireworks idea and Prince agreed that it sounded fun. A few moments passed and I found myself leading a small parade of people (including 2 internationally known recording artists) through the building, into the club area, up the stairs and ultimately ending up on the rooftop of Paisley Park.

With all of the hype in my head leading up to this, I was not let down. We could see probably a dozen or more separate fireworks shows going on simultaneously. It was like nothing I had seen before. Everyone was completely entranced with the experience and it was quite a memorable night. Once the action was over, we all went back inside and continued with whatever we were doing.

After some time passed, the latest Ani DiFranco album was released. In the liner notes "thank you" section, she thanks Prince (actually the symbol) for her favorite Fourth of July. In this same section, called "immeasurable love and gratitude", she mentioned a couple people by name and I got lumped into the "and all at Paisley Park" category.

Like much throughout my Paisley career, I was nameless that night but that's how it was for me. I was fairly quiet and tried to be a hard worker... just the type of guy who falls through the cracks in someone's liner note thank-yous.

7
WHEN AL ROKER CALLED ME SEXY

I used to record every show that Prince played. This
included some rehearsals and sound checks. He would
study these tapes (yes, VHS tapes. This was the late
90's) like an athlete would study game film. If he tried
something new, he would watch the tape and study the
audience reaction. He would make adjustments and
watch the tape again from the following show. He was
truly a perfectionist and this was one of the ways he
was able to put on such an amazing performance.

These tapes were very important to him.
Immediately after a show was over, there would be a
select security guard standing next to me to grab it and
bring it directly to Prince. If there was no security guard,
I would bring it to the dressing room, myself. (I got

really good at avoiding crowds by walking on the tops of chairs when we played theaters). When I got to the dressing room, the bodyguard was usually there to grab the tape. I would not leave it with anyone else except Prince, himself. There were even times when he would watch the performance in the dressing room after the show was over.

He was so serious about his show-tapes that he would even have me record his performances on TV shows. We did The Tonight Show and despite the multi-camera shoot, he still had me record the show for him with his personal camera. I will love to see some of these old personal recordings, once the vault situation is resolved. He also had me record his performance on The Today Show.

I haven't seen The Today Show in years and I'm not sure that millennials know who Al Roker is... I'm not even sure he is still on TV. Whether he is or not, one of the most memorable things Al did was walk around outside the studio and talk the audience that gathered on the street. These were usually tourists, sometimes holding quirky signs representing their state or saying hello to someone back home. Al would put them on TV and talk to them, adding a moment to their 15 minutes of fame.

Another thing that used to happen on The Today Show was their "Summer Concert Series". This was a series of live performances on the street, outside the studios. It was a unique experience when Prince took part in this. We had to show up incredibly early to set up... I think it was around 3:30 or 4a.m. After everything was set up, there was some down-time as the show was going on. We watched a live feed of the show on a giant TV mounted to the side of the building.

Some of the guys on tour thought it would be a good idea to plant a homemade sign in the crowd of fans gathered on the street. This sign was a simple message that said "Griff is sexy"... They thought it would be funny if it got on live TV. So they bribed a girl with a couple guitar picks and had her hold the sign. A little later in the show, Al Roker did a segment right in front of this girl. She handed the sign off to her boyfriend to raise it above Al's head. The entire viewing audience could see the sexy sign... There was a good laugh by some of the crew and I was a little embarrassed but thought it was kind of cool.

Some time passed and Al came outside to do another segment. We were watching this on the giant, outdoor TV when Al told his cameraman and millions of viewers that he was going to talk to the "unsung heroes" of this production... the roadies. I watched the screen as Al started walking through the backstage band gear and road cases. I looked around and saw my fellow crew members jumping and diving out of sight. The next thing I know, Al Roker is directly in front of me and two other crew guys. He's got a cameraman with him and we are now on live, national TV.

He started out talking to the first guy. It was kind of a botched, quick hello. Then it went to the second guy where there was another interaction, as well as my introduction. My buddy pointed me out to Al and told all of America "This is Griff. He's the sexy one". I was completely frozen and scared out of my mind, being on live TV. Al then says "I can see why they call him sexy".

Throughout this entire scenario, I don't think I uttered one word. I actually think I tried to wave but it ended up being very awkward. I said before that I never got much recognition when I worked for Prince... But at least Al Roker scared the shit out of me on live, national TV.

8
WHEN HE CHEATED AT PING PONG

Not long after Prince died, I saw a lot of people tell their stories about the rock star. Some I believed, some I didn't. One of these stories (that I believed) was from Jimmy Fallon. It was about playing ping pong with Prince and losing... Well, guess who else got beat by Prince in ping pong? ... Me.

I had been putting a lot of time into working on his new game room. It was the space directly above the kitchen (it was the wardrobe department when I first started). We added some trendy seating, an old jukebox, colored lighting, a ping pong table, pinball machine and pool table... Prince had also taken a design I drew and inlaid it into the purple carpet. To this day, I still think the design is horrible but Prince liked it. He actually liked it enough to put the design on t-shirts that were sold on tour.

I was working on something in the game room when Prince entered... We were checking out the almost-complete room when he said he wanted to play ping pong. I looked at the purple-felted pool table and told him that I might be a better challenge over there... I can't remember his exact words but he declined. He told me that rich people grow up with pool tables in their homes and in so many words, said that ping pong was more of an every-man's game.

So, I obliged and we started to play, hitting the ball back and forth. It was a fairly competitive volley, then eventually I hit one a little too hard. It was out of bounds and the ball never hit the table. Prince caught the ball instead of letting it hit the ground... a very normal move, just like anyone would do.

Then I noticed something. It happened every time the ball would come close to hitting the edge of the table. He would lean in and snatch it up quickly like it was going out of bounds, without actually letting the ball hit. It was happening over and over again. If the ball was going to land near the white line, we would never be able to see if it would hit the table, or not. He would grab it a split second too early.

In his eyes, the ball was going out of bounds, so he grabbed it. In my eyes, the ball was going to hit the table. He'd catch the ball before either of us knew for sure.

I know the word "cheater" sounds a little harsh and I'm trying to figure out a better way of putting this... but let's just say, Jimmy Fallon... your loss might not be as legitimate as you think.

9
WHEN I TOOK MY ONLY TRIP
INSIDE THE VAULT

I never realized the extent of the fascination with Prince's vault until long after I worked there and after his passing. In five years at Paisley Park, I had only been inside one time... I spent much more time hand-painting the symbol on the door in blacklight paint (which made a 2-second cameo on the local news... I thought was kind of cool).

In order to find the year I went inside of the vault, I had to google which year Red Hot Chili Peppers were on tour with Foo Fighters... it seems that it was the year 2000.

My Paisley buddy and I went to the aforementioned concert at Target Center. Going to a concert when you work in the music business is definitely not like going to a concert like your average ticket holder. Our normal routine would bring us to the backdoor of the venue where we would meet a friend that would issue us passes. After obtaining the passes, we would basically have free reign to walk wherever we wanted, backstage or out in the front of the venue. This would forever spoil me and now I would probably rather not go to a show if it meant sitting in seats like "regular people".

I remember we were waiting at the backdoor when my friend got a call from Prince. The call did not last long but right after it ended he told me "Griff, he's doing something in the vault and wants you to go into work". For some people this would have been the opportunity of a lifetime but I was naive back then. I was more disappointed for getting called into work, right before going to (what I imagine was) a pretty cool show.

I went back to Paisley for the second time that day. I headed down to the vault, which is on the lower, underground level at the studio... the same level as the parking garage. I was met by Prince and he escorted me in. The first thing I remember is him pointing out a pencil drawing. He asked me if I knew who did it. Of course, I didn't... he told me that he drew it. Looking back, this is one of the more cool things that happened out there. Prince knew that I was a visual artist and went out of his way to show me his own visual art.

I asked him if he still draws and he told me no but that he used to enjoy it when he was younger. Here is the most disappointing part of the story. If you ask me what the picture was, I cannot tell you.

There was a time in my life where I tried to block out all of my memories from those days. Those were the memories that used to lead me into bad memories after I left... memories of heartbreak that I wanted to erase from my mind. I guess there are some details that I have lost forever... Also, a couple of drinks before the Chili Peppers/Foo Fighters show, I'm sure did not help.

As I piece things back together, I cannot visualize Prince's drawing. There was also a different occasion where he showed me a painting that Miles Davis personally did specifically for him... and that also is a blank. I think it was space themed.

That hand-drawn Prince picture was in the front room of the vault. We then went into the back part of the vault where I remember seeing aisles of recording reels and the studio engineer sorting through things. Prince had asked me what I had been doing. I told him I was about to go to the concert before I came in... Instead of an apology for pulling me away, he said "Why didn't anyone tell me about it? I would've gone." I shrugged off the question but always thought it was cool that

Prince wanted to go see that show.

Prince left and I wasn't in the vault for long after that. It almost seemed like there wasn't even really any work for me to do. Sometimes I wonder why I was even there... Outside of friends and family, Prince was probably the first person in my life that appreciated me as an artist. Maybe he was simply looking for an opportunity to show me his old drawing... which I will take as a huge compliment.

10
WHEN HE KNEW BLACK LIVES MATTERED

This story takes place on a Monday night. I know it was a Monday night because we went out to see Dr. Mambo's Combo perform at Bunkers... (This group had some former Prince band members and still plays there every Monday). Anyway, some Paisley colleagues and I went to Bunkers for music and drinks. We were there for a little while when Prince happened to show up. It was not uncommon to see Prince there and sometimes he would even get on stage and play.

It was always a little awkward when Prince was around somewhere outside of work. If you hear a story about a former employee hanging out and being best friends with Prince, there's a good chance it didn't happen. There was a lot of walking on eggshells around him and most employees didn't want that feeling outside of Paisley. Most employees generally tried to give him space, if not flat-out avoid him when "out of the office".

Don't get me wrong, there were occasions where he would be fairly social, normal and nice with employees. The first thing that comes to mind is when he rented out the movie theater for everyone to watch Big Momma's House with him... or even the time where we all went to the city park across the street and had a softball game with all the Paisley employees, band members and Prince, himself.

The evening goes on; Prince is in his secluded corner, the band continues to perform and everyone is having a great time. Sometime during the night, the guitar player started playing a Jimi Hendrix inspired Star Spangled Banner. It sounded great and the crowd loved it. Then Prince approached the stage and it looked like he handed the guitar player a note... I wasn't sure if I saw it correctly and questioned myself on missing out on something. The evening continued and at the end of the night, we unexpectedly had to go out to Paisley for a potential late-night party (you were more-or-less on call ALL the time). These parties were normally on a Friday night but a random, different night was not unheard of.

We went back to Paisley (for the 2nd time that day) after bar close and waited to find out whether or not there was going to be a party. It was very quiet and pretty empty at the studio when Prince walked to the back of the building where I was hanging out with one other worker. This was one of the occasions where Prince was very talkative. How the conversation started I don't quite remember. However, I do remember him asking us "Do you know what the note said that I gave to that guitar player?"(I did see what I thought I saw)... Obviously we both answered no. He told us it said "Stop it, you're white"...

Now, before anyone gets bent out of shape, I think it was very clear that Prince was proud of being a black man. I hope you could figure that out by the bass guitar with the black fist on the end of it.

Prince then proceeded to ask us "Do you know why Jimi Hendrix was up on stage at Woodstock playing the Star Spangled Banner?" ... Again, we did not have an answer. He went on to tell us that Jimi Hendrix was playing that song for "all those brothers getting sent to Vietnam to die in a war they knew nothing about"

It was a very unique experience to hear him talk about something so passionately. It was an intimate setting and there was no crowd, there were no cameras or music industry people. It was not a celebrity-stunt to get written up somewhere. It was simply me, one other person and Prince. It felt like this was an issue that he truly cared about and one of the memories I have about him not being a famous musician but a regular guy with regular emotions. It was an occasion where he was teaching a younger generation not only a lesson in rock and roll history but a lesson in general human rights.

11
WHEN I WAS ALMOST A PHOTOGRAPHER FOR YAHOO!

I can't tell you the exact year, however it would have been sometime in the late 90's. I had been working for Prince for a few years... It was long enough where he knew a little bit about me, personally. He knew that I was a visual artist and for some crazy reason, he was one of the few people that had faith in me as an artist. My art was very unpolished and amateurish at the time but he always liked what I did. I am pretty sure that played a factor in why he would do what he was about to do.

He told me that he was doing an interview with Yahoo! Internet Life magazine and there was to be a photoshoot along with it. He said that he wanted me to shoot the photos to go with the interview. All I had to do was call the editor and let her know... Sounds easy, right? Well, not so much.

I called the editor and introduced myself. I told her that I would be the one shooting for the interview. She told me that they have a photographer lined-up and will be using said-photographer. There was no other option. "Okay, thanks for your time. See ya', bye!"

I told Prince that they already have a photographer and that is how it will be. Well, he put the kibosh on that, he told me again that I would be the one taking pictures and to call her back to let her know.

This second phone call was a little awkward. I called her back and told her that Prince insists on having me as his photographer. She was hesitant but became a little more open to this, I guess because she was looking for a successful article with exclusive photos. Here's where the awkward part comes in. She started to ask me about my catalogue of work as a photographer. She wanted to see my portfolio. I had no portfolio and I'm pretty sure my camera was disposable at the time.

I had to regrettably inform her that this would not be an option, to which she became a little confused. She asked "But you are the photographer?" To which I replied yes... "But you don't have a portfolio?!?" You betcha! She immediately told me no again and asked what I was doing even attempting this photoshoot.

I had to try to explain to her that I work for Prince and he wants me to do this. I remember specifically telling her multiple times "You don't understand! He wants me taking these photos" Anyway, after going back and forth with her, the final answer was NO... There is no way she was going to let me ruin this article for her. I kindly obliged and told Prince her answer. Upon receiving this news, Prince told me to call her back one more time and tell her she would be getting stock photos... That's it. End of conversation.

My final phone call was short and sweet. It did not go beyond much of "You're getting stock photos"... I can imagine I sounded young and nervous to this woman. So, maybe she thought I was bluffing and tried to call it... No matter what, that editor and I both learned something that day about what is was like working (or not working) with Prince.

Andrew Kistner

12
WHEN HE GAVE ME 2 SIGNED BLANK CHECKS

I've had a theory that Prince had some trust issues... He never exactly sat me down and told me this... but when you become famous at a young age, I am sure there are a lot of bad people trying to tap into your bank account. He was a little peculiar with his money and over the years, you would hear local news stories about certain vendors or service providers not getting paid... I'm not sure how true or not those were but I never had a single problem with a paycheck. In fact, there were even some unexpected bonuses.

Somehow I became one of Prince's "guys"... There were many people on tour but only a handful that came back to Paisley full-time. These were the guys that

Prince trusted… These were the guys that Prince would call over from across the room to tell something to the person standing next to him.

With that being said, he still seemed just a little nervous the day that I had to go pick up a couple pieces of furniture for him. The pick-up was the easy part… especially for Prince. The tough part for him was paying for it. He ended up giving me 2 signed, blank checks. When he was signing them, he cracked a joke about not ripping him off. However it was one of those "jokes" that was pretty serious… Don't rip him off.

I've seen enough movies to know a lot of extremely fun shenanigans can take place when your eccentric, millionaire boss gives you 2 signed, blank checks. Especially when Chanhassen, at the time still had a small-town feel and I'm sure I could've gotten his bank or mine to give me quite a large amount of cash… But instead of buying a Ferrari and getting in trouble with a mob boss, like a (non-Purple Rain) 80's movie, I followed my orders. The store was on the extreme west side of Uptown, off Lake Street, with the other store a little more towards the heart of Uptown.

I've heard some stories about Prince setting up "stings" to test employee's trust. Most of these had to do with a considerable amount of cash in a random area. Then when said-cash was returned to him, he would let the test subject know that they passed. I've heard a few of these stories throughout the years… Part of me thinks they could have been a true test but yet part of me thinks an eccentric millionaire misplaced a good amount of cash and forgot about it. Then when it was returned to him, he saved face by telling them they passed "the test".

I never found any random amounts of money lying around but Prince knew that he could trust me... Not only with blank checks but with close to 1000 recorded shows/sound checks/rehearsals with no bootlegs made, ever.

Andrew Kistner

13
WHEN HE COPIED MY STYLE

Looking back at my Paisley Park career, one of the coolest things that I got to see was Prince and the band in rehearsals. Not only did I get to see things like Prince cover songs from Bob Marley and Elvis (which I don't think he played in concert) but I also got to see how such amazing live performances came together.

Many times these rehearsals were held in the "club" area of the studio… This is the area where I first started working when I came to Paisley. It's where he would hold his late night parties that sometimes ended between 4 and 5a.m. The stage in this room changed locations a few times over the years but for this particular tour, the stage was placed where you could look through a door into the soundstage (in case you didn't know, Paisley had a soundstage that would rival most Hollywood studios)... As we were getting ready for tour, the soundstage was full of road cases. When you were on the rehearsal stage, you could only see the top of someone's head as they walked through a maze of towering wardrobe boxes.

Sometimes, when I walked through the soundstage and immerged in the club, I would hear the band groan and say something along the lines of "Dang it! Its only Griff"... You see, this was the late 90's and Prince had longer, straight hair... My hair was also long on top, so as I was walking through the soundstage, the band would snap into shape, thinking they are looking at the top of Prince's head coming to rehearsal... Nope, it was only me.

This happened a few times over a number of days. Then one of the band members joked "Griff, you gotta do something about your hair."... So I did.

The next day, before going in, I slicked my hair straight back... It was greased up, shiny and slicked flat against my head, Pat Riley style... I went on with my day then it came time for rehearsals.

What happened next was one of the most bizarre coincidences in my entire life. Still, as I write this, I have a hard time believing it happened... This day where I randomly decided to do my hair in a way that I never had before, Prince showed up with his hair slicked back.

I am not kidding. I had never seen him do it before. I had never again seen him do it after... Obviously this was quite noticeable by everyone, as I walked past the stage, Prince said into the microphone "Hey Griff, nice hair".

Prince was notorious for turning over staff but for some reason I lasted longer than many people... Perhaps showing up prepared on "slicked back hair day" made him think we were on the same wave length.

Andrew Kistner

14
WHEN HE SENT ME TO SCHOOL

I was at Paisley Park during somewhat of a unique time. The Purple Rain days were over a decade behind us and the studio worked with a skeleton crew. Not having too many people on the payroll meant that as an hourly employee, your tasks could be almost anything and you spent a lot of time working directly with Prince.

What this environment meant for me was that Prince would eventually know a little about me, personally. He knew that I am a visual artist who loves to create and draw. One of my favorite things to do at Paisley was to assist the art director when he came to town. I had worked on many photo shoots as well as music videos. A couple of my drawings ended up on t-shirts and he had seen enough from me to recognize me as an artist.

There was one day when I ended up walking with a small group of people, Prince included, through the atrium. As we were moving along, out of nowhere Prince looked at me and said "Griff, I want to see what that wall looks like if it were painted blue". I never really found out exactly which wall he was talking about because my first thought was something along the lines of "Huh? Wait... What?

Hardly a moment passed and I asked him how we were supposed to that. He said "It's easy, you just put it in the computer... Do you know how to do that?" I told him no and he instantly said "You need to learn how to do that. You need to go to school"... I don't recall his exact words but he said that he would pay for it.

Well, he wasn't kidding... There was one of those for-profit colleges a couple cities away and I got enrolled. The accounting office gave me a check to cover my class and that was my first experience with Photoshop. At the time, I really didn't appreciate that gesture as much as I should have. Looking back, it was one of the more generous things a boss has done for me and I probably should have taken a little more advantage of it.

Yes, you've heard stories about Prince sometimes being difficult guy with whom to work. I won't deny that there were challenging times but I'll keep those stories to myself... No matter what the challenges, there were always times like this where Prince wanted me to reach my full potential. I am the first to say that my art back then lacked experience and honestly, was not all that great... However, he saw something in me where he knew I had potential.

My life after Prince had a bit of a downward spiral but I climbed out being a much happier and wiser person... Life is good today but I never found my career in art. Outside of family and friends, Prince has been the only person who really had faith in me doing art. I still enjoy painting as a hobby and through the entire course of my life can say that Prince had a direct influence on me as an artist.

Andrew Kistner

15
WHEN I MADE HIM A BASKETBALL COURT

One of the fun things at Paisley Park was setting up and working the big events. I was there for the Emancipation release party, which was his first release free form the record label... I was there for "Rave Un2 The Year 2000", the pay-per-view event that had Prince welcome in the new millennium... Also, the event where I met 90's MTV icon Bill Bellamy... Yep, that's how prestigious these events were.

The big one that almost did not happen was a party for the 2000 NBA draft that was being held in Minneapolis (according to Wikipedia, one of the worst in NBA history).

There was a company that wanted to host an NBA

draft party at Paisley Park. It was going to be a star-studded party with a DJ and full basketball court in the soundstage. It was always exciting anticipating an event like this. Then out of nowhere, the company pulled out and the event was cancelled. Maybe they found out how far away Paisley is from Downtown Minneapolis? No one really knew what happened but then some time later, word came down that Prince still wanted to host a party. He also still wanted the basketball court.

Someone was able to arrange portable hoops and balls but that was it... Somehow I got the task of the actual "court"... No instruction... Just "Hey Griff, he wants a basketball court and we need it by tomorrow." That's it... Go ahead, Griff... Get going. This was all part of the job. There were weird requests that came up all of the time and we just had to make them happen.

This took place in a time before smartphones and a time before easily accessible internet. I was trying to figure out how to build a basketball court, overnight. I went into the back office at Paisley and called a friend to have him look up the dimensions, then had to brainstorm... By this time, I think it was about 8p.m. or so... I was thinking back to my school days about the lines on the gym floor and for some reason I got the idea to try vinyl tape... I went to the hardware store and made sure I had plenty. Once I got back, I started measuring and taping. This project was taking forever and I was going to be in for an all-nighter.

Sometime in the middle of the night, I had the lines taped off. I took it upon myself to add a logo in the middle, like a real basketball court. It never really crossed my mind how risky this was. Prince was a very particular guy and honestly, there was a chance he would not react well to my artistic rendition of his symbol as a logo in the middle of the court.

So, there I was, painting the stylized Prince symbol in the center of my homemade basketball court, with a boombox next to me and in walks Prince. It had to be somewhere around 4a.m. He walked up to me and looked at the unexpected logo. He didn't say whether or not he liked it, which was a good thing. Because if he did not like it, he would have said so instantly and had me paint over it. The only thing he asked me is "Who is this?" referring to the CD I had playing...

By the way, employees were sometimes weird about the music they played while at Paisley. They wanted to be sure that it was something Prince would like and would approve of... Well, I thought Prince was gone, so I was playing whatever I wanted to play.

To Prince's "Who is this?" I responded that it was a band called Fishbone. I'm not sure if he was familiar with the band or not but sometime later on tour, he had Fishbone's trombone player come up on stage and play during a show... I'd like to think that he was unfamiliar and I'm the guy that introduced him to the band.

After a long night, the basketball court was finished. I got home sometime in the morning and was back to work in the afternoon. The party went off fine and Prince, yet again had an unrealistic request completed on time... a basketball court installed "by tomorrow".

Sometimes the crew at Paisley seemed just short of miracle workers.

16
WHEN I THOUGHT PAISLEY PARK WAS HAUNTED

If you had to ask me if I believe in ghosts, I might have to tell you "No"... However part me thinks there's a chance.

We live in a time where almost everyone has a camera on them at every waking (and sleeping) moment... but there is one thing that has not increased: credible pictures of ghosts. Practically anything that comes out is almost immediately debunked. If that isn't reason enough, most stories you hear are of ghosts dressed in Victorian Era clothing. Almost everyone sees the romanticized version of specters... When's the last time you heard of someone seeing a ghost dressed in a Wham! T-shirt?

Lastly, the ghost hunting shows that were such a trend a few years back, with all of the latest technology, never really captured solid evidence… These people have dedicated their lives to proving that ghosts exist… They spend the night in a haunted house, convinced that they just missed capturing a real ghost on camera… They were so close! You'd think they couldn't wait to get that one convincing picture… Then when morning comes, they pack up their gear and go home, telling us how close they were to getting convincing evidence… but maybe next time.

So, as you can see, I'm a bit of a skeptic… One of the only places I thought something could be a little paranormally hairy? Paisley Park.

During the day with people around and all the lights on, it was fine… The tricky part was when you were the last one to leave. You would have to walk to the front of the building to turn off all the lights, then proceed through the dark building, set the alarm in back and exit through the wood shop. This task could potentially take place at any time throughout the night. Let's say it's 3 a.m. and everyone's gone. The large building is eerily quiet except for a couple doves and some random creeks and pops made by this massive structure.

It's easy getting to the front of the building. It's easy turning the lights off. It's easy once you start your trek to the back. Then, about halfway through the atrium area I would get an eerie feeling. By the time I got to the little nook where they kept Isis the cat's litter box, I would feel like there was something on top of me. If I looked any other direction than straight ahead, I was going to see something horrifying... Every time, I wanted to spin my legs like Scooby Doo and run out of that building as fast as I possibly could.

I never did run and I never actually saw anything... But coming from a guy who doesn't exactly believe in ghosts, an empty Paisley Park in the middle of the night was one of the spookiest places I've ever been in my life.

I have brought this up to other former employees and no one else had ever felt it. The logical part of me has always said this was an overactive imagination... However, my overactive imagination tells me it was something seriously, paranormally sketchy.

Andrew Kistner

17
WHEN I ASKED FOR A RAISE

All throughout Prince's career, there were urban legends about him being a challenging employer... Sometimes it's hard to say which were true and which were just legends. A lot of these stories ended with Prince firing someone.

I had been at Paisley for about three years. It was not like a "regular" company. There was no HR department. There was no annual performance review with your supervisor... In fact I was in a spot where I had seen so many supervisors come and go that it got to a point where I didn't really have someone to which I reported. This was difficult when I realized I had been there that long without a raise. I started to ask around and I had a few people say they would go to bat for me but it just never happened. This is because of those urban legends... There were stories about people being let go after they asked for more money.

I had more-or-less exhausted all my resources in asking for a raise. So, one day I decided I would just take matters into my own hands. I would ask him, myself. Prince's presence and his persona were very powerful and intimidating by default. I knew he valued his time and that, along with the urban legends is why I got a little nervous to ask him this tough question.

I made my plan and I would catch him the moment he got in. I would not give him time to start anything... I knew he had arrived from the sound of the motion sensor alarm on the camera pointed at his garage door. I waited by the now-infamous elevator and as soon as he got off, he walked to the front desk. I caught up and stopped him. I felt very awkward but stuck to my plan. I had his full attention and told him that I had been working there for three years and I literally used the phrase "I'm strapped for cash. Can I have a raise?"

Without hesitation he said yes. I was a little shocked. This went way easier than anticipated; I thanked him and asked who I should talk to... He said "I'll take care of it".

Later that day, I was paged to the accounting office where I was told Prince wanted to give me a raise. I was an hourly employee and it was a very generous hourly raise. I honestly couldn't tell you what I was expecting when I asked Prince for a raise but I can say that I was prepared for anything, including getting fired... and that's what it took to work for Prince: Be prepared for absolutely anything.

18
WHEN HE TOOK A DOUBLE FLUSHER

It was not unusual to work late-nights at Paisley Park... I am not talking about "Hi honey, I'm going to be a half-hour late for dinner"... I am talking about get there at 10am and do not leave until 5am the next morning. This story takes place on one of those late nights.

It's late. I'm not sure what time...probably anywhere between 10pm and 2am. I am walking towards the front of the building and Prince steps off the elevator. He stops me and tells me "Griff... Umm, there is a plumbing problem in the upstairs bathroom. It's the middle stall"... My first thought was about how much it would cost for an after-hours plumber. Yes, Prince was a millionaire but I had enough experience out there that I knew he would not like the cost an emergency plumbing bill.

I proceeded to check out the situation. As I'm walking up the stairs, I'm not exactly sure what to expect... I had an open mind and realized that "plumbing problem" could mean countless things. I wasn't sure if I'd be ankle-deep in water that was gushing out of an overflowing toilet. I'm a pretty creative guy, so the imaginary scenarios got pretty sketchy on my short walk up the stairs.

Upon entering the bathroom, I was a little relieved to find out everything seemed normal. I opened the middle stall to find... well, sorry to put it so bluntly but Prince-poop in the toilet along with some toilet paper. The toilet was not running. Everything seemed fine, so I used my public-bathroom-foot-flush and decided to see what happens.

I'm not sure if you've ever run into toilet issues but there are multiple things that can happen when you flush a toilet with "plumbing problems". To my surprise, everything went down with no problems. I waited until it stopped running again and flushed one more time. Everything checked-out fine.

Later in the evening (or I guess possibly morning), I ran into Prince and he asked me if the bathroom was fixed. I told him yes and then he asked what was wrong. I told him "I just flushed it again"... The look on his face reminded me of a person on a quiz show when they buzz in, then freeze up as reality hits when they don't know the answer.

... Then he turned around and left.

I'm not exactly sure what moral you can take from this story... just know that no matter who you are... a lumberjack or an international music legend. You are not so special that everything in life goes down exactly the way you want it to the first time. This holds true in life, love and... I'm sorry... poop!

Andrew Kistner

19
WHEN HE WROTE A SONG ABOUT ME

I first started at Paisley Park when I was a 19-year-old kid. I had to grow up fast, learning to live on a tour bus with 5 to 11 other guys who were all veteran roadies (and didn't have much time for showing the ropes to a new kid). It was unlike anything my small town had to offer and I was learning on the fly what it was like to be on tour.

Eventually, we settled-in with a good crew of guys working directly for Prince that would take me under their wing and show me some of the ins-and-outs of touring. If you are wondering about the first rule of touring and think it has to do with band gear, equipment or how to pack, you're wrong.

Believe it or not, the first rule of living on a tour

bus is: no number 2's in the bathroom. It is set in stone and literally the first thing that I (or any rookie) was told. Maybe there have been tour bus bathroom improvements since then but 15 years ago it was the golden rule.

Another thing that I was told by multiple people was to get out... That is, to get out of the business before I got sucked in too far where I could no longer get out. The veteran roadies said to have fun and do it for a while but don't make it a life-long career. I didn't really care what anyone had to say because I was 19 and knew everything. However, I would slowly learn what they meant.

When you are gone for months at a time, it can be difficult having a healthy home-life. For the first time in my life, I missed my family Christmas because I was an ocean away in Germany. It also puts tensions on relationships because you almost had to have your life dedicated to the job... It took me five years to figure that out when I started to talk to my then-girlfriend about quitting.

This was at a time where Prince started giving me art director duties. I was not qualified for the position but like I stated in some other stories, he liked my art and wanted to give me a chance. He had me working on a lyric book for an album called The Rainbow Children. I had gotten to work at about 10am and put in a long day until 8pm when Prince stopped in to check out the progress. He took a look and said that I could call it a day and head home.

I did, indeed go home where I lived with some other Paisley employees. It was around 1am when my roommate got a call from Prince and he handed me the phone. Prince was asking me why the lyric book was not done. I remember telling him "We talked about this. You told me it was looking good and I could go home." I'm not sure how the conversation ended but I went back to Paisley to finish the project.

Before I left, I told my girlfriend that this is the night I'm going to quit. I got back to Paisley at 1:30 in the morning. Prince let me in the side door and I headed up to the art director office. After some time, Prince came in to chat. He started talking about the art projects we will be working on after the lyric book. At this point, I gathered all the courage I had and told him I will finish the book but I am done after this... Prince looked at me and asked "Done, as in quit?"

I'm not sure if everyone has this experience but I can exactly pinpoint a moment in my life where I chose between two completely different paths... it was when Prince asked me if I was quitting.

I told him "Yes... Done, as in quit". He asked me what I was going to do. I did not tell him it was because of a girl. I told him that I was driving a piece of crap car, didn't have a lot of money and I wanted to really make something of myself. He immediately interrupted me and said "That's why we're doing this!". There was a concern in his voice but I didn't care. I was too much in love to realize the opportunity he was giving me.

He asked me what I was going to do. I told him that I was going to attend school full-time... "For what?" he asked. I told him that I was going to study animation. "In Minnesota!?!? There's no animation in Minnesota!" I didn't care what he had to say. I was going to put Minnesota on the map for animation.

I eventually moved out of the house with the Prince employees and was talking to my new roommate as he pulled up The Rainbow Children album online. We listened to the first few seconds of each track until we got to number 13, "The Everlasting Now"... this song sounded different, so we listened a little longer. The first line of the song says "I knew this dude, he was very cool, he used to rule, until he went to school". It was a peculiar feeling because this is the exact conversation we had when I quit. I had the phone number to the studio sound engineer who did this album. I immediately called him and asked if that song was about me. He said yes, it is.

My animation dreams fizzled out as my then girlfriend proved to me that I was in love with wrong person. My trust was broken... I hit rock bottom and rediscovered myself as an artist.

Fast-forward to the present and life is good... Now, as a middle-aged, slightly overweight, married man, I will always have a reminder that a guy like Prince thought I was cool (even if he said it in the past tense) I know he wouldn't say that about just anyone.

20
WHEN I GAVE UP ON HIM

After reading a few of these stories, you'll figure out that when I was younger, Prince was ready to give me a chance. A chance at something I am very passionate about... ART.

After five years working for him, he gave me my biggest opportunity doing my first "art director" project ... then I quit. I told him that I was leaving to go out and make something of myself and it sounded like he wanted me to stay. He wanted to help make me into something. That project was going to be the first of many but unfortunately I did, indeed quit that night.

I never tried to stick around or get back in with the Prince camp. In the following 15 years, I saw Prince only twice. The last being only 6 months before he died. I'd be lying if I said the reunion went well but in his defense, I left him abruptly just as he was giving me a major opportunity.

Now, as a middle-aged man, I still have a passion for art. I look back to see that I've never had another opportunity to do art for a living. I've always had support through family and friends but when you're dealing with an artist-ego, you have a little voice that tells you those people are obligated to support you... Outside of that "obligated" group, Prince was the only person that was willing to give me a chance at being an artist... If I lived five more lifetimes, there's a chance that an opportunity like this would never present itself again... and I walked away from it.

I hit some lows after leaving Prince and my artwork evolved. Some people say it turned a bit "dark". Being dark was never an intention during this time but I'm sure it showed. I learned that creating art was a very necessary outlet for me. I could not have climbed out of those low points without it. I have never stopped making art.

Throughout the years, I've shown paintings here-and-there, mostly at coffee shops and bars. It is always difficult putting those pieces in public, as they are my heart and soul displayed for everyone to see. Sometimes I wonder what Prince would have thought if he saw exactly what I turned into as an artist... Deep down I know he wouldn't have exactly cared. I learned that from our last meeting... However I will always carry with me that someone who was such an iconic figure trusted me and knew that I have the ability to do some amazing, creative things with my art.

Andrew Kistner

ABOUT THE AUTHOR

Andrew Kistner, aka Griff spent 40 to 80 hours a week working for Prince. This went on for over a half-decade when he made the decision to quit. Throughout this time, he met many people that came and went from Paisley Park, including some lifelong friends. Without all of these friends and acquaintances, Griff's stories from Paisley would not be the same.

Being young and naïve during his time at Paisley, it was not until after Prince passed that Griff realized just how many people he had touched through his music.

Unlike some former employees, Griff cannot post social media photos hanging out with celebrities and being backstage at events... Fate led him down a different path. What he can do is share his stories from working very closely with the music icon

88044211R00059

Made in the USA
Lexington, KY
05 May 2018